Critter Crafts & Recipes

Compiled by
Michele Reyzer

Illustrated by
Joyce Mihran Turley

muddy boots™

we jump in puddles

Lanham · Boulder · New York · London

Milk Jug Feeder *by Michele Reyzer*

Invite some feathered friends to your yard with this recycled bird feeder.

WHAT YOU NEED

empty gallon milk jug

nail or hole punch

green acrylic paint

craft glue

wire

clear non-toxic craft glaze

leaves, twigs, pebbles, and pinecones

birdseed

WHAT YOU DO

1. For the main entrance to the feeder: Draw and cut out a large circle (about 2½ inches wide) a few inches up from the bottom of the jug.

2. For the perch: Make a small, twig-sized hole just below the large one, either with a nail or hole punch. (See step 5 for adding the perch.)

3. Brush green paint on the outside of the jug and let it dry. Glue leaves onto the outside of the jug.

4. For the hanger: Punch a hole through both sides of the top of the jug, just below the cap, and slip a wire through it.

5. For the roof and final touches: Glue a dozen or so twigs to each side of the jug's top, as shown. Poke a thicker twig into the perch hole. Glue on pebbles, pinecones, or any other decorations you like. Paint over the leaves with craft glaze.

6. Add birdseed and hang your feeder from a tree branch. (Be sure to put it where you can easily refill it.)

Now sit back and wait for the birds to discover the newest diner in town!

Edible Nest *by Ellen Lambeth*

Here's how to build a robin nest that's good enough to eat.

WHAT YOU NEED

12-oz. package of butterscotch or peanut butter baking chips

5-oz. can of chow mein noodles

blue jelly beans or Jordan almonds

2 cookie sheets

saucepan and spoon

wax paper

WHAT YOU DO

1. Stir baking chips in a pan over low heat until melted and smooth.

2. Stir in noodles until completely covered.

3. Plop 8 to 10 spoonfuls of mixture onto cookie sheets covered with wax paper.

4. Shape each spoonful into a cup-shaped nest.

5. Put in the refrigerator to chill.

6. Add several candy "eggs" to each edible nest.

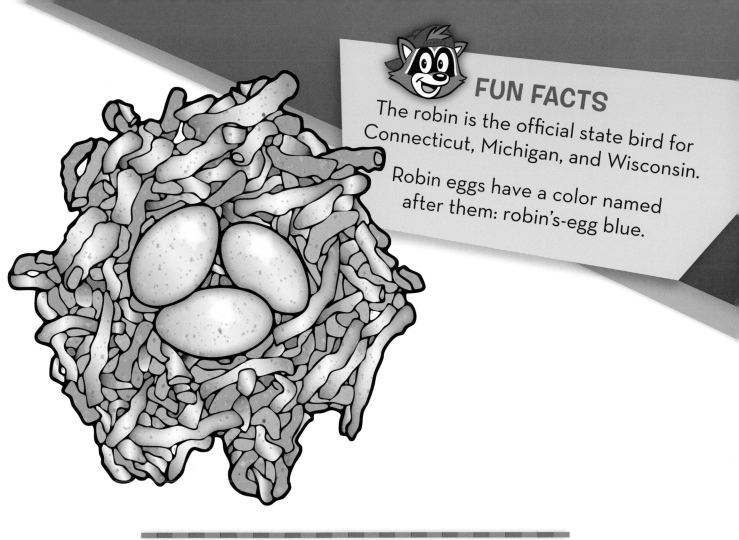

ROBIN RIDDLES

How do robins find their way to their nesting places?
They follow the "egg-sit" signs.

What's a robin's favorite part of the newspaper?
The crossWORM puzzle.

Butterfly Sandwich
by Laura Blankenbaker

You'll go buggy over this tasty butterfly snack.

WHAT YOU NEED

slice of bread

stalk of celery

raisins

cream cheese
(colored pink with food coloring)

WHAT YOU DO

1. Cut a slice of bread into two triangles. Put the triangles in the freezer for 15 minutes so it will be easier to spread the cream cheese on them.

2. Spread the cream cheese on the two bread triangles.

3. Cut a stalk of celery to make the butterfly's body. Spread cream cheese on the piece of celery.

4. Cut thin strips of celery to make antennas.

5. Arrange bread triangles, celery body, and antennas in the shape of a butterfly.

6. Decorate the butterfly's wings and body with raisins.

Coffee Filter Butterfly

by Ranger Rick® staff

Transform a coffee filter into a beautiful butterfly that won't flutter away.

WHAT YOU NEED

washable markers

coffee filter

spray bottle filled with water

7 mini pom-poms

craft glue

clip clothespin

pipe cleaner

WHAT YOU DO

1. Use the markers to draw a design on the coffee filter.

2. Place the coffee filter on paper towels and spray lightly with water. Set aside until it is dry.

3. Glue pom-poms on the flat side of the clothespin to make the butterfly's body.

4. Wrap the pipe cleaner around the middle of the coffee filter to make the butterfly's wings.

5. Clip the coffee filter and pipe cleaner with the clothespin. Bend the pipe cleaner to make the butterfly's antennas.

Strawberry Ladybugs *by Michele Reyzer*

This "berry" sweet treat is easy to make—and fun to eat!

WHAT YOU NEED

strawberries

blueberries

mini chocolate chips

string licorice

toothpicks

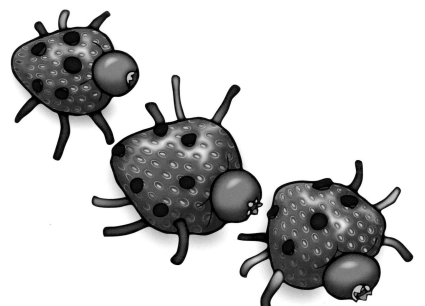

WHAT YOU DO

1. Wash a strawberry and remove the stem and leaves.

2. For the ladybug's head, push a toothpick into the top of the strawberry, leaving about half an inch sticking out. Put a blueberry onto the toothpick.

3. For the ladybug's spots, press the pointed ends of some mini chocolate chips into the strawberry.

4. For the legs, push six small pieces of licorice into the strawberry, as shown.

Ladybug Pals
by Ranger Rick® staff

Some people think ladybugs bring good luck.
See how lucky you are when you make a whole bunch of them.

WHAT YOU NEED

medium-sized
pom-poms
(red, orange, yellow)

small black pom-poms

black felt

black pipe cleaners

googly eyes
(two for each ladybug)

craft glue

WHAT YOU DO

1. Cut a pipe cleaner so it measures 3" long. Bend the cut piece into a "V" shape.

2. Glue the bottom of the "V" shape between one medium pom-pom and one small pom-pom. Hold together for 60 seconds to allow the glue to stick.

3. For the spots, cut tiny circles out of black felt. Glue them onto the ladybug's back.

4. Glue two googly eyes onto the ladybug's head.

5. Bend the tops of the pipe cleaner to create antennas.

Geckos On the Go *by Michele Reyzer*

Making colorful geckos can be fun from the get-go!

WHAT YOU NEED

lightweight cardboard, such as a cereal box or file folder

craft paint or crayons

small suction cups or magnets

WHAT YOU DO

1. Draw the outline of a gecko on a piece of cardboard, and cut it out. (See gecko shapes at right.)

2. Use craft paint or crayons to decorate the gecko with colorful designs, as shown.

3. To display your gecko on a window or refrigerator, glue small suction cups or magnets onto its belly.

Frog Salad
by Laura Blankenbaker

You'll jump for joy when you taste this frog-tastic salad!

WHAT YOU NEED

green lettuce

green apple

2 cucumber slices

black olive

grape tomato

WHAT YOU DO

1. Fold a large lettuce leaf in half and place on a plate.

2. Cut the green apple into eight wedges. Then position four of the wedges next to the lettuce to make the frog's legs, as shown.

3. Cut small triangles out of two of the apple wedges to make the frog's feet.

4. Place the cucumber slices above the lettuce to make the frog's eyes.

5. Cut the black olive in half and place on the cucumber slices to make the frog's eyeballs.

6. Cut a "smile" shape out of one of the apple wedges and cut the tomato in half. Place these on top of the lettuce to make the frog's mouth, as shown.

FUN FACT

Frogs are some of the best jumpers in the animal kingdom. They can leap more than 20 times their own length!

FROGGIE FUNNIES

Why are frogs good baseball players?
They catch a lot of flies.

What did the frog do when it heard a funny joke?
It croaked up.

What do you get when you cross a rabbit with a frog?
A bunny ribbit.

Where do city frogs live?
In pond-ominiums.

Egg Carton Turtle

by Ranger Rick® staff

Shell-ebrate turtles by making this recycled egg-carton craft.

WHAT YOU NEED

cardboard egg carton

green paint
(two different shades)

green construction
paper or craft foam

googly eyes

craft glue

WHAT YOU DO

1. Cut one cup from the egg carton. Paint the outside of the "shell" cup with one shade of the green paint.

2. Cut two rectangles (1 ½" x 3 ½") out of construction paper or foam to make legs. To create toes, snip two small triangles into the ends of each leg.

3. Cut one rectangle (1" x 4") from the paper or foam. Trim one end to make a pointy tail and round off the other end to make a head.

4. When the cup is dry, use the other shade of green paint to make designs on the turtle's shell.

5. Once the shell is completely dry, glue the legs, tail, and head to the bottom rim of the egg carton cup, as shown.

6. Glue googly eyes onto the head.

Fruity Sea Turtle *by Michele Reyzer*

You'll dive into snacktime when *this* seafood is on the menu!

WHAT YOU NEED

pineapple

orange

grape

toothpick

dried black-eyed peas

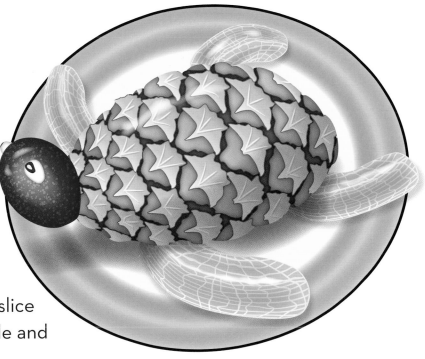

WHAT YOU DO

1. For the turtle's shell, cut a slice from the rind of a pineapple and place it on a plate.

2. Arrange four peeled orange-segment flippers under the "shell."

3. For the head, attach a grape to the pineapple with a toothpick. Press two black-eyed pea eyes into the grape. (You can also use other items for eyes, such as raisins, nuts, or chocolate chips.)

Fan-tastic Faces
by Michele Reyzer

Keeping cool is a breeze with one of these wild fans.

WHAT YOU NEED

wooden craft stick or paint stirrer

two egg-carton cups

sturdy paper plate

colorful craft paint

craft glue

magazines with photos of wildlife

yarn or fake fur (optional)

strong packing tape

Put your creation to use and show everyone that you're a "fan" of wildlife!

WHAT YOU DO

1. Paint the wooden stick, egg-carton-cups, and one side of the paper plate. (Use any colors you like.)

2. After the paint has dried, glue the egg-carton cups to the plate, as shown.

3. Look through magazines and cut out features such as eyes, ears, nose, and mouth.

4. Glue cut-out eyes to the tops of the egg-carton cups. Arrange the other cut-outs on the plate to create a face, then glue in place.

5. If you want, add yarn, fake fur, or other decorative touches to the plate.

6. Tape the wooden stick to the back of the plate.

The Prickly Pair *by Michele Reyzer*

Don't toss your old socks—turn them into a no-fuss cactus garden!

WHAT YOU NEED

old sock

plastic-foam ball

plastic grocery bags (optional)

rubber band

green paint

flower pot

pebbles
(enough to fill pot)

googly eyes

craft glue

toothpicks

construction paper

WHAT YOU DO

1. Push a plastic-foam ball into the toe of a sock. (The sock should fit snugly around the ball.) For a tall cactus, add plastic bags or other stuffing after the foam ball. Wrap a rubber band around the sock to keep everything tightly in place.

2. Paint the sock green. You may need several coats of paint. (Or use a green sock and skip this step!)

3. Once the paint has dried, place the sock in the pot, then fill the pot with pebbles.

4. Glue on googly eyes. Break the toothpicks in half. Press the pointed ends into the sock until it's covered with "spines."

5. Cut flower shapes from construction paper. Stick them on a few of the toothpick spines, as shown.

Sand Dollar Pancakes *by Laura Blankenbaker*

You'll feel like you're at the beach when you make—and eat—these two fun treats!

WHAT YOU NEED

pancakes
(Prepare them using your favorite pancake mix.)

cream cheese

toothpick

WHAT YOU DO

1. Make pancakes. Allow them to cool slightly.

2. Spread a thin layer of cream cheese on each pancake.

3. Using a toothpick, draw the sand dollar design in the cream cheese, as shown.

Crab-Apple
by Michele Reyzer

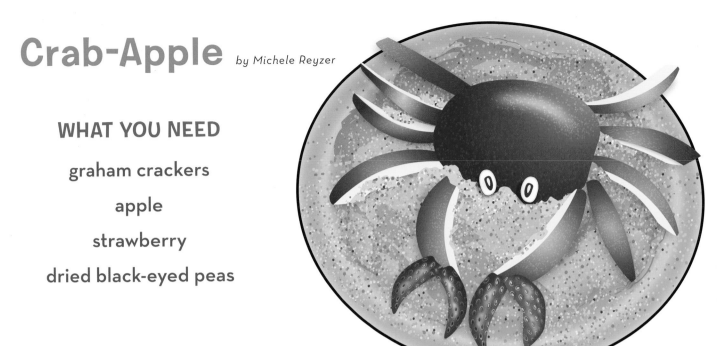

WHAT YOU NEED

graham crackers

apple

strawberry

dried black-eyed peas

WHAT YOU DO

1. For "sand," crush some graham crackers and sprinkle them on a plate.

2. Cut an apple in half and place one half on the crumbs, cut side down.

3. Cut the other half of the apple into 10 slices for the legs and arrange them around the crab.

4. For the claws, cut four slices from a strawberry and place them next to the two front legs, as shown.

5. Press two black-eyed pea eyes into the apple. (You can also use other items for eyes, such as raisins, nuts, or chocolate chips.)

Flying Fish *by Michele Reyzer*

With just a plastic bottle or two, you can add a touch of the tropics to your room.

WHAT YOU NEED

plastic water or soda bottle

small nail

fishing line or nylon thread

stapler

acrylic paint

googly eyes

craft glue

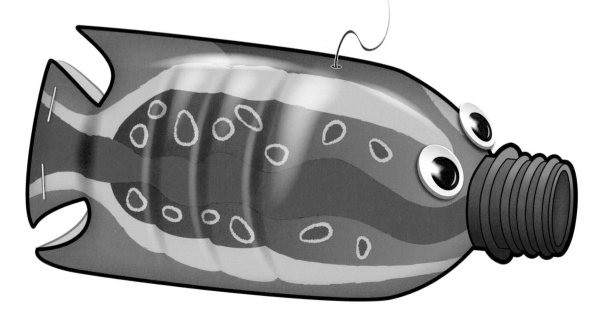

WHAT YOU DO

1. Remove the cap and label from an empty, clean bottle. Cut the bottom off the bottle.

2. Punch a hole with a small nail in the top of the "head" of your fish. Poke a long piece of fishing line or nylon thread through the hole and tie a knot on the inside end.

3. Pinch the open end of the bottle so the two sides meet and staple them together in the middle. Cut out fins and a tail around the staples, as shown.

4. Paint colorful fish patterns on the bottle. Once the paint has dried, glue on googly eyes.

Now hang your fish up. Or make some more and turn them into a mobile!

Sea Star Pretzel *by Lori Collins*

This pretzel looks like it came from the salty sea!

WHAT YOU NEED

1 package of active dry yeast

1 ½ cups of warm water

¾ teaspoon of regular salt

1 ½ teaspoons of sugar

4 cups of flour

1 egg

2 tablespoons of coarsely ground salt

WHAT YOU DO

1. Stir the sugar and regular salt in the water. Then gently mix in the yeast. Allow the mixture to sit for five minutes until the yeast begins to foam.

2. Slowly stir in the flour a little at a time until a dough forms. Knead the dough until it is elastic (about two minutes).

3. Break off a piece of the dough and roll it into a long rope. Cut the rope into 2-3" long pieces. Put five pieces together to make a sea-star shape. Place the pretzels on a cookie sheet.

4. Lightly beat the egg in a bowl. Brush the beaten egg over the pretzels using a pastry brush. Sprinkle each pretzel with coarsely ground salt.

5. Bake pretzels at 400°F for 25 minutes.

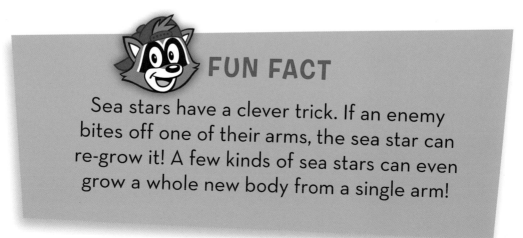

FUN FACT

Sea stars have a clever trick. If an enemy bites off one of their arms, the sea star can re-grow it! A few kinds of sea stars can even grow a whole new body from a single arm!

Go Fish! *by Laura Blankenbaker*

After one round of reeling in a match, you'll be hooked on this fishing game!

WHAT YOU NEED

stick

2' string

paper clips

10 index cards

round magnet
(the kind with a hole
in the middle)

piece of blue poster board

construction paper
(different colors)

WHAT YOU DO

1. Cut the poster board to look like a pond.

2. Tie the string to the stick. Tie the magnet to the other end of the string.

3. Cut 10 fish shapes out of construction paper. Put a paper clip on each fish. Write a different number on each fish, and put all the fish in the pond. Write the corresponding words for those numbers on the index cards.

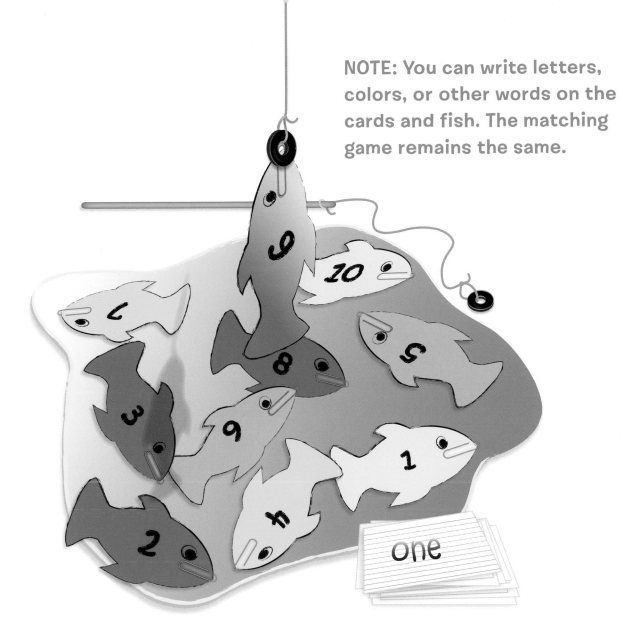

HOW YOU PLAY

Children take turns picking an index card. Then they use the fishing pole to "fish" for the corresponding number.

Camping is a great way to get outside and enjoy nature. Here are some fun activities for your next family campout.

Shadow Puppets *by Michele Reyzer*

Put on a play in the dark with these easy-to-make shadow puppets.

WHAT YOU NEED

construction paper

hole punch

glue or tape

wooden craft sticks

flashlight

WHAT YOU DO

1. Cut animal shapes out of construction paper.

2. Use a hole punch to give the animals eyes or a design.

3. Glue or tape the animal shapes onto craft sticks.

4. Shine a flashlight against a wall of your tent. Hold the puppets in front of the light so that they cast shadows. Act out your story with the shadows.

Nature Telescope

by Laura Blankenbaker

There is a lot to see and observe when you're camping. This telescope will help you focus your eye on nature near your campsite.

WHAT YOU NEED

empty paper towel tube

empty potato chip can with plastic lid

construction paper

markers or crayons

glue and tape

12 inches of ½-inch wide ribbon

WHAT YOU DO

1. Cut the bottom off the potato chip can and an "X" shape in the plastic lid.

2. Wrap the chip can and paper towel tube with construction paper. Tape to hold in place.

3. Decorate both tubes with markers or crayons.

4. Glue a piece of ribbon around the bottom of the chip can and the top of the paper towel tube.

5. Carefully slide the paper towel tube through the "X" shape in the plastic lid.

Whoooo's Hungry? *by Laura Blankenbaker*

If you're looking for a healthy way to start your camping day, this breakfast owl fits the bill!

WHAT YOU NEED

English muffin

peanut butter

2 slices of bananas

2 raisins

"O"-shaped cereal

slice of American cheese

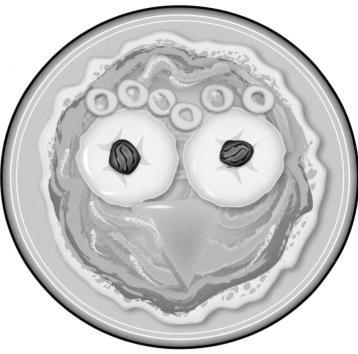

WHAT YOU DO

1. Spread peanut butter on the English muffin.

2. Use banana slices and raisins to make the eyes. Place the cereal above the eyes, as shown.

3. Cut a triangle shape out of the cheese and place under the eyes to make a bill.

Trail Mix *by Ranger Rick® staff*

Rustle up some trail mix to take on your next campout.

WHAT YOU NEED

4 cups of "O"-shaped cereal

1 cup of nuts (peanuts, almonds, pecans, walnuts, or a mixture)

½ cup of raisins

½ cup of dried cranberries

½ cup of M&M-type candies

sealable plastic bags

WHAT YOU DO

1. Measure all the ingredients and mix them together in a bowl.

2. Divide the mixture into serving-size portions and put in sealable plastic bags.

Published by MUDDY BOOTS
An Imprint of The Rowman & Littlefield Publishing Group, Inc.
4501 Forbes Boulevard, Suite 200, Lanham, Maryland 20706
www.rowman.com

Unit A, Whitacre Mews, 26-34 Stannary Street, London, SE11 4AB
Distributed by NATIONAL BOOK NETWORK
The National Wildlife Federation. © 2016 All rights reserved.
Craft illustrations © 2016 Joyce Mihran Turley.

Book design by Katie Jennings Design
The National Wildlife Federation & Ranger Rick contributors
Mary Dalheim, John Gallagher, Greg Hudson, Ellen Lambeth, Hannah Schardt, Kathy Kranking,
Michele Reyzer, Lori Collins, Cindy Olson, Susan McElhinney, Robyn Gregg, Chris Conway,
Deana Duffek, Michael Morris, Kristen Ferriere, David Mizejewski, Maureen Smith

Thank you for joining the NATIONAL WILDLIFE FEDERATION
and MUDDY BOOTS in preserving endangered animals and
protecting vital wildlife habitats. The National Wildlife Federation
is a voice for wildlife protection, dedicated to preserving America's
outdoor traditions and inspiring generations of conservationists.

Library of Congress Cataloging-in-Publication Data Available

ISBN 978-1-63076-210-0
ISBN 978-163076-211-7 (electronic)
Printed in the United States of America